Theme park science

FALLING FOR FUN

By Nathan Lepora

ticktock

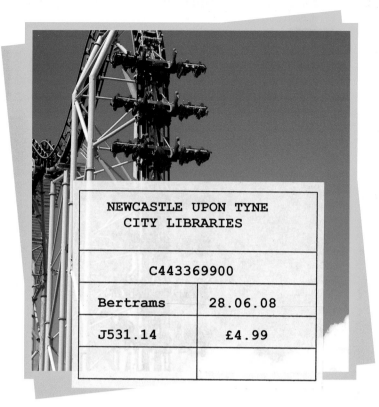

First published in Great Britain in 2008 by ticktock Media Ltd,
2 Orchard Business Centre, North Farm Road, Tunbridge Wells, Kent, TN2 3XF

ticktock project editor: Sophie Furse
ticktock picture researcher: Lizzie Knowles
ticktock project designer: Hayley Terry
With thanks to: Carol Ryback, Justin Spain and Suzy Gazlay

ISBN 978 1 84696 613 2 pbk

Printed in China

Picture credits (t=top; b=bottom; c=centre; l=left; r=right):
Robb Alvey www.themeparkreview.com: 4, 16c. Adam Bailey/ Action Plus: 8. Cedar Point: 25. CJM Photography / Alamy: 17. Kitt Cooper-Smith / Alamy: 10/11 main. Illustrations by Justin Spain: 6, 22, 25, 28-29. Ira Chaplain/ Rex Features: 21 inset. Chad Ehlers/ Stock Connection/ Rex Features: 22/23 main. Andrew Fox/ Alamy: 5. Jeff Greenberg/ Science Photo Library: OFC. Robert Harding Picture Library Ltd/ Alamy: 13. iStock: 14. Noah K. Murray/ Star Ledger/ Corbis: 21l. M. Timothy O'Keefe/ Alamy: 9. Roger Ressmeyer/ Corbis: 12c. Shutterstock: 2, 3, 6/7, 11 inset, 18, 20/21 background, 20bl, 26/27, OBCtr x2. Superstock: 1. Illustrations by Hayley Terry: 10c, 16b. Ticktock Media Archive: 20tl. www.ultimaterollercoaster.com: 15.
US Department of Energy/ Science Photo Library: 19.

Every effort has been made to trace copyright holders, and we apologise in advance for any omissions. We would be pleased to insert the appropriate acknowledgments in any subsequent edition of this publication.

CONTENTS

Roller coasters could not work without **gravity**. It pulls roller coaster cars, people, and everything else toward Earth. The force of gravity also causes objects to accelerate, or **speed** up, as they fall to the ground.

WHAT IS GRAVITY?

Everything on Earth, living or not, feels the force of gravity. Gravity holds rocks to the ground. It helps you take a step or jump from a tree. If gravity stopped working, matter such as rocks, water, animals, and even you, would float off into space.

Gravity is a constant, one-way force that pulls objects toward the middle of Earth. Imagine digging a hole in the United Kingdom, and one in Australia. If you dropped a ball down each hole the balls would keep falling until meeting each other at Earth's core!

DROP COASTERS
You can feel what falling is like by riding a drop coaster. These rides are the steepest of any roller coaster. A vertical track drops the coaster straight down.

Oblivion at Alton Towers, UK, was the first drop coaster in the world. The ride hurtles down and into a gaping hole in the ground.

WHAT GOES UP . . .

Everyone knows that what goes up must come down. When a roller coaster climbs up a hill, you know it will come whooshing down again very soon.

As roller coaster cars fall, they roll along twisting tracks. The tracks guide the falling cars through loops and turns. Then – just before you hit the ground – the track takes you back up again.

Gravity speeds up a car
rolling down a hill

Speeding
up

GRAVITY

Gravity slows down a car
going up a hill

Slowing
down

GRAVITY

GRAVITY AND ACCELERATION

Gravity makes falling objects fall faster. So, a falling object gains speed because of gravity. The change in speed is called **acceleration**. As an object moves upward, gravity also pulls down on it. The object slows – this is called **deceleration**.

Roller coaster cars do not have motors. Their speed is controlled by the slope of the tracks. Going downhill, roller coasters accelerate until they zoom past the lowest point along the track.

Climbing the next hill, the cars decelerate until they crawl over the top, ready for the next thrilling drop.

Hills and dips on a roller coaster work by using gravity.

THAT'S AMAZING!

A roller coaster on the Moon would be really boring. The Moon's weak gravity would make the ride fall very slowly.

On a roller coaster, your weight feels like it keeps changing. But you know that your body stays the same. Instead, other **forces** push on you during the ride to make your **weight** feel different.

WEIGHTY FORCES

When you lift something, you fight against gravity. Your muscles provide the force to lift an object. At the same time, gravity pulls the object back to the floor. This heavy feeling – which is actually the pull of gravity on an object's **mass** – is its weight.

Mass gives objects weight. The mass of an object is how much substance or 'stuff' makes it up. A stone has more mass than a cube of sponge that is the same size. Gravity pulling on an object's mass gives it weight.

A weight-lifter struggling against gravity

Imagine if the pull of Earth's gravity suddenly halved in strength. The mass of everything would stay the same, but everything would weigh half as much.

DID YOU KNOW?

Scientists do not measure weight in **kilograms**. Mass is measured in kilograms. Weight is a force and should be measured in **newtons**.

ILLUSIONARY WEIGHT

Imagine you are sitting on a roller coaster. As you go over a hill, you feel lighter. Shooting through a dip, you feel heavier. You have the thrilling feeling that your weight keeps changing.

You feel light going over a hill . . .

A person's weight pulls them down.

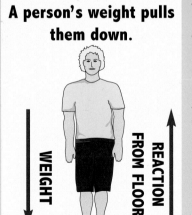

WEIGHT

REACTION FROM FLOOR

This sensation that your weight changes on a roller coaster is just an illusion. Your weight never changes because the pull of gravity stays the same.

Quicksand is not solid and so cannot push against gravity.

WEIGHT

NO REACTION FROM FLOOR

What you really feel is the reaction of the seat against your body. A roller coaster travelling up a hill pushes your seat against you. You feel this force squashing your insides. The sensation of being squashed fools your brain into thinking you weigh more.

Similarly, a roller coaster accelerating downhill makes you feel lighter. You are lifted off your seat. Your insides seem to float as they 'unsquash'.

. . . and you feel heavy going through a dip.

THAT'S AMAZING!

Italian mathematician Galileo Galilei (1564-1642) measured how gravity causes acceleration. He dropped various sized cannon balls off the Leaning Tower of Pisa. He discovered that different masses fall with the same acceleration.

G-force measures the force on your body from acceleration. **G-force** is equal to the force of gravity. In zero g-force, you feel weightless.

G-FORCE

Every time you change speed or direction, a force pushes against you. These are the forces you feel with every twist and turn of a roller coaster. Scientists call them g-forces.

One g is the normal weight you feel from gravity. Roller coasters can give forces of more than four g. These forces make you feel four times heavier.

Fighter pilots are trained in special machines (above) so they get used to how g-forces feel

Fighter planes turn at almost ten g. Their pilots feel ten times heavier than normal!

BEST COASTER SEATS

Most people think the best seats are at the front of a roller coaster. Those seats give you a great view of the bends and loops as you hurtle towards them.

Some coaster fans prefer the back seats, though. That is because the coaster cars in the back accelerate the most – you feel more of the thrilling g-forces!

Thrill-seekers enjoying the effects of g-forces.

FREE FALL

An object is in **free fall** when it drops with gravity. The only force acting on a freely falling object is its weight. Sky divers are in free fall when they jump out of planes.

Free fall makes you feel weightless. Normally you feel the reaction of the ground against you. This force goes into your body squashing your insides. When you free fall no forces push against you. You feel as if your stomach and insides float up. It's very strange!

THAT'S AMAZING!

The **weightlessness** of free fall is the same feeling that astronauts have when they float in space.

A parachute traps air and slows the skydiver's fall to Earth.

AIRTIME

Free fall on a roller coaster is called **airtime**. You feel airtime when the car shoots over a hill or drops straight down.

Superman: The Escape has the longest airtime of any coaster today. The ride shoots up 126 metres and then drops to Earth. While in free fall you feel weightless for over six seconds!

Superman: The Escape at Six Flags Magic Mountain, California, USA.

Some theme park rides create their thrills by toppling toward the ground. How they fall depends upon where their **centre of gravity** is located. This centre point is where an object's weight is concentrated.

BALANCING

Weight feels like it is centred inside an object. For example, you must find the middle point of a ruler to balance it on one finger. This balancing point is the ruler's **centre of gravity**.

Objects topple if their centre of gravity is unstable. Imagine trying to balance the ruler on one end. It wobbles and falls – the ruler's centre of gravity is not supported in the proper place.

TOPPLE TOWER

The topple tower at the Bellewaerde Theme Park in Ieper, Belgium, is a great ride that falls over – to the shock of everyone on it. Riders sit on a spinning disk that is raised up a huge tower. The tower then topples over and bounces back up while looping around and around.

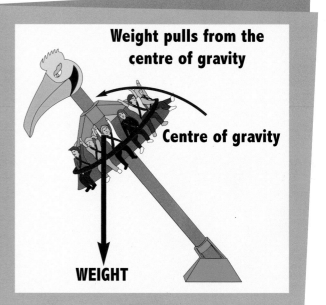

Weight pulls from the centre of gravity

Centre of gravity

WEIGHT

DID YOU KNOW?

Your body's centre of gravity is somewhere within your hips. You can only balance when your centre of gravity is above your feet.

Energy causes things to happen. Roller coasters move, bombs explode, objects fall, fire burns, and the Sun gives us light, all because of **energy**.

WHAT IS ENERGY?

Everything in the universe happens because of energy. Energy makes things work. Without energy, nothing can happen.

Something that loses its energy cannot do anything. Roller coasters grind to a halt without energy. Fires cannot burn, bombs do nothing, and lightning fizzles out without energy to power them.

This fire is giving off light and heat energy

The enormous energy of a nuclear bomb with its famous mushroom cloud.

STORING ENERGY

Energy can be stored to use later. Saved energy does not do anything while in storage. When the energy escapes it makes things happen. For example, a bomb gives out its energy when detonated in an enormous explosion.

THAT'S AMAZING!

Exploding stars, or supernovas, release more energy than our Sun produces in ten billion years.

TYPES OF ENERGY

Energy comes in many different forms. These forms depend on what the energy is doing.

Heat energy is the energy you feel when something is hot. You need heat energy to stay alive – otherwise you would freeze.

Electrical energy causes electricity to flow. Most gadgets around the house are powered by electrical energy.

Potential energy is a form of energy that is stored. An object has potential energy when it is up in the air. This energy can be released later as kinetic energy.

Kinetic energy causes objects to move. Fast objects like speeding roller coasters have lots of kinetic energy.

Light energy is the energy you see when something glows. The Sun makes enormous amounts of light energy.

Kinetic energy is a form of energy from movement. Fast objects have lots of kinetic energy.

WHAT IS KINETIC ENERGY?

Anything that moves has kinetic energy. An object with no kinetic energy is completely still. The faster an object moves the more kinetic energy it has.

Kinetic energy depends on both mass and speed. It is easier to make a small object move because it needs less kinetic energy. A jumping flea might be very fast, but it has very little kinetic energy.

At the bottom of a hill the coaster has the most kinetic energy

Fast speeds

The faster a roller coaster goes, the more kinetic energy it has.

COASTING ON ENERGY

Roller coaster cars weigh several tonnes and hurtle along at awesome speeds. Because of these large masses and speeds, the coaster cars have huge amounts of kinetic energy.

A coaster car gains kinetic energy as it speeds down a hill. The pull of gravity accelerates the car to faster and faster speeds.

THAT'S AMAZING!

A roller coaster's kinetic energy is similar to that of a thousand people running.

Roller coasters must store lots of potential energy to go fast. Objects positioned at a height store potential energy. When they fall, the potential energy changes into kinetic energy.

WHAT IS POTENTIAL ENERGY?

Everyone knows that things speed up as they fall. But where does this kinetic energy come from?

It takes energy to gain height. You use energy when climbing stairs because you must pull yourself up against gravity. This energy is not lost. It is stored away as potential energy that can be regained later – by sliding down a bannister, for example.

Potential energy is energy waiting to be put to use. If you let an object fall, its potential energy changes into kinetic energy.

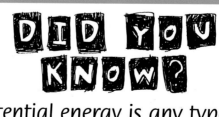

DID YOU KNOW?

Potential energy is any type of stored energy. Stretched elastic bands and compressed springs also store potential energy.

The height of this roller coaster gives lots of potential energy.

STORING ENERGY

Hills on a roller coaster ride are designed to store potential energy. A strong motor tows the coaster up the first hill. At the top, the car has lots of potential energy. Larger hills store more potential energy, which provides the fastest rides.

At the top of the hill, the roller coaster has the most potential energy

Speeds slow as kinetic energy decreases

HEIGHT

Roller coasters keep swapping kinetic and potential energy as they speed up and slow down. The term for describing how energy changes from one form to another is called **conservation of energy.**

SWAPPING ENERGIES

Energy can help you understand why things happen. For example, where does the kinetic energy of a moving car go when it **brakes**?

Friction from braking turns kinetic energy into heat energy. You feel this heat from friction when you rub your hands together. Car brakes can heat up to temperatures of 315°C in a sudden stop!

Going up and down hills swaps potential energy with kinetic energy.

Some of the energy of a roller coaster gets used up as heat or sound energy. But energy is never destroyed – even as it changes form. The same amount of energy still exists. We say energy is conserved.

DID YOU KNOW?

Most electrical energy comes from burning coal, oil or gas. Some scientists say we are using these faster than we can replace them.

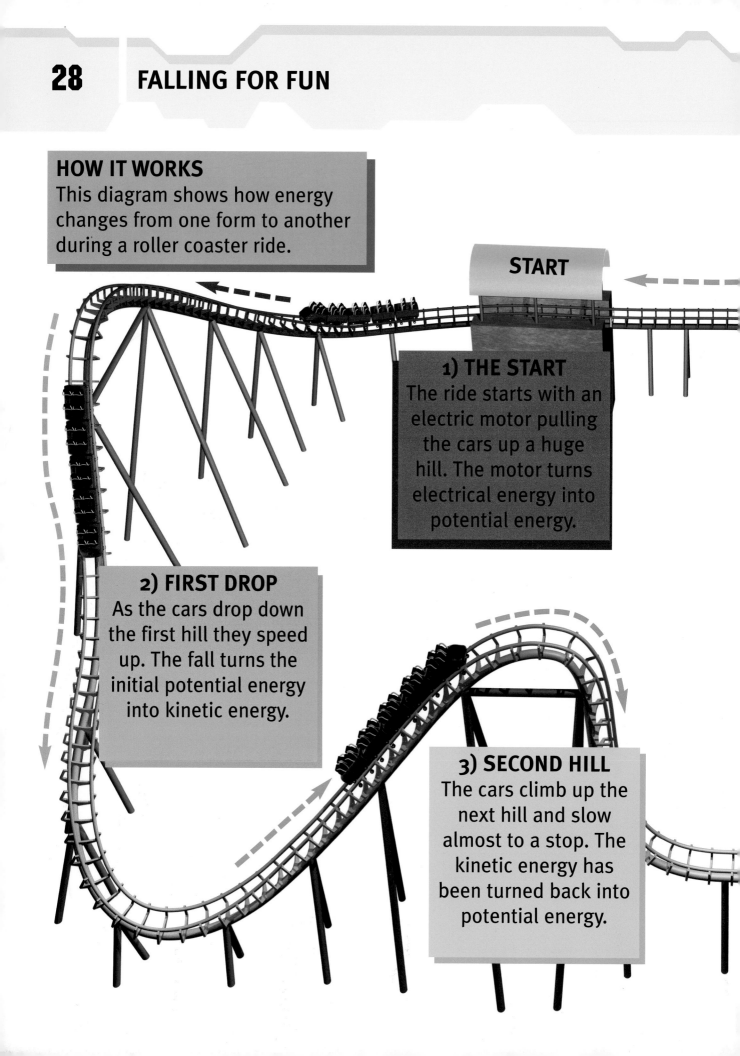

HOW IT WORKS
This diagram shows how energy changes from one form to another during a roller coaster ride.

START

1) THE START
The ride starts with an electric motor pulling the cars up a huge hill. The motor turns electrical energy into potential energy.

2) FIRST DROP
As the cars drop down the first hill they speed up. The fall turns the initial potential energy into kinetic energy.

3) SECOND HILL
The cars climb up the next hill and slow almost to a stop. The kinetic energy has been turned back into potential energy.

5) BRAKE RUN

The ride ends with the cars braking and coming to a stop. The last remaining kinetic energy turns into heat energy.

4) LOOPS AND BENDS

Then, the cars travel the loops and turns of the ride. Their potential energy and kinetic energy keep swapping back and forth throughout the ride. However, the cars also lose energy to friction.

Acceleration is a change in speed as time passes. An object that is gaining speed is accelerating. An object whose speed is decreasing is decelerating.

Airtime is the feeling of being weightless on a roller coaster. (*see also weightlessness*)

Brakes are devices that use friction to slow or stop an object. (*see also friction*)

Centre of gravity is the point where an object's weight is concentrated. (*see also weight*)

Conservation of energy is the principle that energy can never be created or destroyed, but only turned from one form into another.

Deceleration is a decrease in speed over time; the opposite of acceleration. (*see also acceleration*)

Electrical energy is a type of energy that causes electricity to flow. (*see also energy*)

Energy is the ability to make something happen. There are many forms of energy.

Forces are pushes or pulls that change the shape, speed, or direction of an object.

Free fall is when an object drops with just the force of gravity.

Friction is a force that resists movement. Rough surfaces cause higher amounts of friction than smooth surfaces.

G-forces measure the forces on your body from acceleration. One g is the same as the normal weight you feel from gravity. *(see also gravity)*

Gravity is the force that pulls one mass towards another. It also causes objects to accelerate as they fall toward Earth.

Heat energy is the energy in heat. *(see also energy)*

Kilograms are the units in which mass is measured.

Kinetic energy is a type of energy from movement. *(see also energy)*

Light energy is the energy in light. *(see also energy)*

Mass is the amount of substance an object has for its size. Mass causes an object to resist acceleration.

Newtons are the units in which forces such as weight are measured.

Potential energy is a type of energy that is stored. *(see also energy)*

Speed is how fast an object moves.

Weight is the pull of gravity on an object's mass. *(see also mass)*

Weightlessness is the feeling you have in free fall or in space. *(see also free fall)*